The
MOUSSE/SOUFFLÉ
Cookbook

The MOUSSE/ SOUFFLÉ Cookbook

by Patricia Holden White

HOLT, RINEHART AND WINSTON

New York   Chicago   San Francisco

*Published simultaneously in Canada by Holt, Rinehart and
Winston of Canada, Limited.*

ISBN: 0-03-002011-5
Library of Congress Catalog Card Number: 72-80207

FIRST EDITION

Designer: Mary M. Ahern
Drawings by: Donald Leake

Printed in the United States of America

FOR
Deborah

Contents

PART ONE | GENERAL INFORMATION

1. Introduction 3

2. Decorating Mousses and Soufflés 13

3. Sauces for Mousses and Soufflés 17

4. Keeping Mousses and Soufflés 21

PART TWO | RECIPES

5. Savory Mousses and Soufflés:

Poultry, Seafood, Meat 25

6. Cheese Soufflés 41

7. Vegetable Mousses and Soufflés 49

8. Sweet Mousses and Soufflés 57

INDEX 77

Part One

GENERAL INFORMATION

1

Introduction

MOST PEOPLE wouldn't dream of putting mousses and soufflés in the category of convenience foods. The glory of a fully risen soufflé is often relegated to the dinner table of someone else, who, it is rumored, studied under a great chef, or to the favorite French bistro around the corner. And a beautifully garnished mousse is seldom to be seen outside of a cold buffet at an elegant restaurant. Admittedly, soufflés are never to be kept waiting when ready, but in all other respects they are really easily made, and indeed at least half of their preparation can be done well in advance of actually popping them into the oven. And mousses are splendid catchalls for leftover meat, vegetables, and fruits.

Basically, a hot savory soufflé is composed of a white sauce, enriched by egg yolks, flavored by the addition of seafood, vegetables, meat, cheese, or whatever, and made to rise by the addition of stiffly beaten egg whites and the application of heat. A cold sweet soufflé is based on the same principle of suspending an egg yolk or cream mixture in beaten egg whites, but as it is not cooked, the stabilizing process is accomplished by the addition of gelatin rather than heat. Mousses differ from soufflés in that they are denser and do not always use whole eggs. They do not rise nearly so high as soufflés when hot and keep better when cold than do cold soufflés. They are simply richer and heavier, where soufflés are lighter and airier.

The basic rules for soufflé- and mousse-making are simple, but must be followed exactly for optimum results. Let us take soufflés first.

The first thing to calculate before making a soufflé is your oven. The evenness in oven temperature is extremely important in making soufflés, just as it is in baking. As you cannot open the oven to check your soufflé while it is cooking, your oven must have an even temperature throughout. The best way of testing this is to buy a roll of refrigerated slice-and-bake cookies, cut them evenly, and bake. Take them out as the directions instruct and have a good look at the difference between those baked at the back and those at the front. If the back ones are black and the front one pale, you've got oven troubles. Get the oven adjusted, as it will affect all your baking.

Now, soufflé dishes come in many pretty designs; they are always round, of various circumferences, and generally from two to four inches deep. They have straight sides which help the soufflé to rise properly.

It is not necessary to use a soufflé dish, as any straight-sided oven dish will do, but do use a round rather than an oval dish to assure that the soufflé is completely cooked through and hasn't any soft spots in the middle.

There are a number of people who think that soufflé dishes, whether being used for hot or cold soufflé-making, should always have a collar made to fit them. This, I think, is completely unnecessary in the case of hot soufflés, as a properly made soufflé will puff perfectly without having to be contained by a collar. Also, having to remove a collar from a hot soufflé means risking the soufflé's losing some of its height before it gets to the table through spending time in getting the collar off. Collars are necessary for cold soufflés that are going to be decorated, as what you decorate are the crown and sides of the soufflé that come out above the top of the dish. The easiest way to make a collar is with aluminum foil. Make a strip (use one piece doubled over to make it stiff) larger than the circumference of your dish. Place it around the top of the soufflé dish, overlapping the dish at the bottom by at least 2 inches for stability and extending about 3 inches above. Secure with a paper clip (metal, if the soufflé is to be baked) at the top and with a piece of string halfway down the foil, where the rim of the dish is. Secure gently. Butter the

inside of the collar with melted butter and a pastry brush (if you insist on using a collar for a hot soufflé) or with vegetable oil and a pastry brush for a cold soufflé. The shortening will make it easier to take the collar off without the soufflé sticking to the foil, and it will also help the sides of a hot soufflé to brown.

The inside of the soufflé dish should always be buttered or oiled, depending on whether you're making a hot or a cold soufflé, lightly but thoroughly.

Equipment you will need will include a double boiler, at least two large bowls, an egg beater or electric mixer, a whisk of medium size, a good scraper for folding in egg whites, measuring cups, and measuring spoons. Do not use aluminum bowls, as they have been known to turn egg whites gray. Glass, Pyrex, and enamel bowls are preferable. You may also need, depending on the recipe you choose, a grater, a coarse sieve, a food mill or electric blender, and a large pan filled with hot water.

The making of a soufflé up to the point of adding stiffly beaten egg whites can be done in advance, and this part of soufflé-making is very stable. The prima donna of soufflé-making is the egg white, as once beaten, it must be added to the egg yolk mixture instantly and the soufflé popped into the preheated oven without a moment's waiting. Some of the recipes that follow call for the baking dish to be set in a pan of hot water. Most of these soufflés are a bit denser than those baked on their own and have a slightly more custardy texture.

All utensils used in soufflé-making must be spotlessly clean and completely free of grease before starting. Even a bit of grease on the bowl in which egg whites are beaten will deter the whites from being beaten to their fullest.

A word about eggs: Always use large to extra-large eggs. As you will see, most of the recipes call for one more egg white than egg yolk, which seems to be the optimum proportion for fluffy, yet rich, soufflés. Eggs, you will find, separate easiest when cold, but egg whites beat highest when at room temperature. So, separate your eggs when cold, prepare the egg yolk basis for the soufflé, and then beat the egg whites just before popping the souffle into the oven. The white of egg should always be beaten in a completely clean, dry bowl, as mentioned before. If a bit of egg yolk does get into the white, get it out before beating. The height of the soufflé depends on this, as the beating of egg whites until they are stiff and shiny, but not dry, is what gives the soufflé height. If you use a rotary or electric mixer, lift it in and out of the egg whites while beating to get as much air into the mixture as possible.

Care should be taken in folding the egg whites into the egg yolk mixture. This must be done deftly and quickly, making sure that no large areas of egg white remain. Every moment you spend in folding the two mixtures together makes the soufflé lose some of its air, so fold the mixtures quickly, with long strokes, rather than hysterically chopping at it. To ensure a crown arising from the middle of your soufflé, quickly run a knife around the soufflé one inch from the side, making a trough, mounding the excess soufflé mixture into the center.

Once into the preheated oven, the soufflé is on its own. NEVER OPEN THE OVEN DURING BAKING or you will have a pudding, not a soufflé. And when the appointed moment arrives to take the soufflé from the oven, whisk it to the table. You may keep your guests waiting—never your soufflé.

Mousses, as I've said, are soufflés' richer cousins. Like the custardy type of soufflés, many hot mousses are baked in a dish set in a pan of hot water to keep them moist. Most mousses are made in molds, either ring molds or molds of decorative shapes, and un-molded before serving. Simple cold mousses can be made and served in glass dishes, rather than being unmolded.

Where the soufflé dish was buttered or oiled, so the mold for mousses is either rinsed in cold water or oiled before adding the mousse mixture. Where a clear mousse is wanted, rinse in cold water, as oil will sometimes blur the surface of the mousse. The basic cold mousse mixture is then poured into the mold and chilled until firm.

Unmolding a cold mousse is best accomplished by reversing the mousse mold over a serving plate and pressing a hot cloth over the surface of the mold. The mousse will soon plop onto the serving plate, ready to be filled or decorated before serving. Should you want to do this well before serving, be sure to put the unmolded mousse back in the refrigerator. Hot mousses can be unmolded by allowing them to set for up to five minutes after they have been taken out of the oven, then running a knife around the outside of the mousse, and reversing the mold over a serving plate. A whack on the bottom of the mold will help to remove the most reluctant mousse.

When making cold mousses, you might want to think about which ingredients sink or swim in a gelatin-based mixture, in order to get the prettiest effect. Fresh apples, bananas, fresh strawberries, marshmallows, walnuts, almonds, and coconut will swim; while fresh oranges, grapes, and most canned fruits will sink. The level in the mold at which various additions to your mousse will suspend themselves depends on their own density. Do not use fresh or frozen pineapple (canned is fine) when using gelatin, as it inhibits the gelatin from doing its job.

And speaking of gelatin: gelatin must always be completely dissolved before added to any mousse or soufflé. Otherwise the undissolved residue is gritty or rubbery and the over-all result is dreadful. One tablespoon of gelatin will stiffen about two cups of liquid. All cold mousses must be chilled for at least three hours to allow the gelatin to do its job properly.

I would never recommend freezing a mousse that has gelatin in it, as the result is likely to be irretrievably rubbery.

2

Decorating Mousses & Soufflés

HOT SOUFFLÉS should be rushed to the table without embellishment in all their own glory. Hot mousses are often made in a ring mold and, after having been unmolded, are filled with creamed or buttered vegetables, creamed chicken, or simply a profusion of watercress or parsley.

But cold soufflés and mousses provide a creative wonderland. If a cold soufflé has been made with a collar, this collar should be gently removed. Gently, so as not to pull away any of the soufflé that now stands proudly above the rim of the dish. If you are going to decorate, please, please don't do so in a hot kitchen. Your mousse or soufflé will not in all likelihood dissolve into a puddle before you, but heat around it will not be conducive to either its texture or its tenacity in holding the decorations pressed upon it.

Cold sweet mousses and soufflés with whirls of stiffly whipped cream pushed out of a pastry bag, sprinkled with chopped nuts and shaved bitter chocolate, are sure to set your guests cheering. Or a strawberry mousse or cold soufflé with halves of fresh strawberries pressed into the top and sides is terribly impressive. I find that using an old pair of tweezers, sterilized, to place nuts, etc., into the sides of a cold soufflé makes the job quite easy. Savory cold soufflés and mousses can be decorated best with slices or curls of peels of raw vegetables, or bouquets of watercress, parsley, and radish roses.

3

Sauces for Mousses & Soufflés

A COLD SAVORY soufflé or mousse is best served with a mayonnaise-based sauce, with perhaps some chopped chives or curry powder added. As these mousses and soufflés tend to be made of a number of ingredients, the accompanying sauce should be simple, but piquant enough to bring out the best flavor in the mousse or soufflé.

With simple sweet soufflés, such as vanilla or coffee, try a zabaglione sauce (3 egg yolks, 1 tablespoon sugar, $\frac{1}{4}$ cup of Marsala, 1 tablespoon brandy, whisked together in the top of a double boiler).

With chocolate soufflés, a rum sauce (2 egg yolks, 3 tablespoons sugar, $\frac{1}{2}$ cup whipped cream, 2 tablespoons rum, 1 teaspoon vanilla, whisked together in the top of a double boiler).

For liqueur soufflés, such as kirsch or cointreau, a fruit-jam sauce ($\frac{1}{2}$ cup fruit jam and $\frac{1}{4}$ cup water heated together for 10 minutes, strained, and with the addition of 2 tablespoons of same liqueur as soufflé).

For all sweet soufflés, heavy cream to which $1\frac{1}{2}$

teaspoons of brandy extract and granulated sugar to taste have been added.

Or simply heavy cream or a generous dusting of confectioners' sugar.

For flaming soufflés, pour 2 tablespoons of warm brandy over the top of the soufflé and light just as you are ready to serve.

4

Keeping Mousses & Soufflés

Hот soufflés, needless to say, do not keep and certainly can never be reheated with any degree of success. Once a soufflé begins to lose the air that makes it so magical, its Cinderella days are over and it becomes rather puddinglike rapidly.

Hot mousses are more stable and can be reheated, but in reheating will most probably lose some of their texture. Although it can be done, I would not recommend reheating mousses.

Cold soufflés lose more in keeping than cold mousses, because they are basically airier than mousses, particularly if the cold soufflé has been partially eaten. Gelatin tends to get a bit rubbery over the passage of a day or so under refrigeration, and beaten egg whites lose air and so the soufflé loses its lightness. Cold mousses, being heavier than cold soufflés, keep better, particularly if the mousse has been made in individual serving dishes. But for the maximum in texture and flavor, two days covered in the refrigerator should be the longest time to keep a cold mousse.

Part Two

RECIPES

5

Savory Mousses & Soufflés

POULTRY | SEAFOOD | MEAT

COLD DUCK AND ORANGE MOUSSE

This is a very rich mousse, tastiest when garnished with fresh orange slices.

Type of dish: 1½ quart mold, or ring mold, rinsed in cold water

Serves 6

2 tbsp. butter	⅓ cup white wine
2 tbsp. flour	¼ cup orange juice
1 cup milk	1 tbsp. brandy
1 tbsp. minced parsley	½ cup heavy cream, whipped
1 tsp. seasoned salt	3 egg whites
¼ tsp. white pepper	orange slices or Mandarin oranges, watercress for garnish
pinch of dry mustard	
2 cups cooked duck, minced	
2 tbsp. plain gelatin	

Whisk together butter and flour until smooth over medium heat. Add milk, parsley, seasonings and keep whisking until thickened and smooth. Remove from heat and stir in minced duck. Soften gelatin in wine, then dissolve by setting dish in a pan of hot water. When dissolved, add orange juice and brandy. Beat egg whites stiffly and add with whipped cream to the duck and melted gelatin, folding together quickly. Pour into mold and chill. Unmold and garnish with oranges and watercress.

COLD POULTRY MOUSSE

This is the ideal solution for what to do with roasted chicken, turkey, or duck. The mousse tiest made in a ring mold, filled with cut-up f... or cold marinated vegetables.

Type of dish: 1½ quart mold, oiled

Serves 4–6

1½ cups milk
3 egg yolks, beaten
1½ envelopes plain gelatin
¼ cup white wine
½ cup clear chicken soup
1¾ cups cooked chicken, coarsely ground
1 tsp. seasoned salt
½ tsp. seasoned pepper
dash Worcestershire sauce
3½ ounce package sliced almonds
1 cup heavy cream, whipped

In a double boiler, combine milk and egg yolks, cooking over hot water until smooth and thick. Remove from heat. Add gelatin to white wine to soften. Heat chicken soup and add to gelatin mixture, stirring until dissolved. Add to egg mixture. Then add chicken, seasonings, and almonds, and lastly fold in whipped cream. Pour into ring mold and chill.

COLD CHICKEN CURRY MOUSSE

Type of dish: 1½ quart ring mold, oiled
Serves 4–6

1 envelope plain gelatin
¼ cup white wine
1 can vichyssoise
1 tbsp. curry powder (adjust to personal taste)
1 tbsp. freeze-dried chives

2 cups cooked chicken, ground
1 cup heavy cream, whipped
½ tsp. seasoned salt
½ tsp. seasoned pepper
½ cup chutney

Soften gelatin in white wine. Heat vichyssoise and stir softened gelatin into it. Continue stirring until gelatin is completely dissolved. Add curry powder, chives, chicken and set aside to cool. When cooled add stiffly whipped cream, salt, pepper, and chutney. Fold together and pour into oiled mold and chill until firm. Unmold and fill ring with cold rice salad mixed with mayonnaise and cubed cucumbers, with a dollop of chutney on top.

CHICKEN SOUFFLÉ

Oven temperature: 350 degrees

Type of dish: 2 quart soufflé dish, buttered

Serves 4–6

3 tbsp. butter	1 tbsp. parsley, chopped
3 tbsp. flour	1 tbsp. freeze-dried chives
¾ cup milk	5 eggs, separated
¼ cup brandy	1 egg white
½ tsp. seasoned salt	2 cups cooked chicken (or turkey) meat, coarsely ground
¼ tsp. white pepper	
¼ tsp. dry mustard	
dash Worcestershire sauce	crumbled bacon for garnish (optional)

Combine butter and flour in a saucepan, or in the top of a double boiler, and whisk until smooth. Add milk and continue whisking until thickened. Add brandy, seasonings, parsley, and chives. Drop egg yolks in one at a time, whisking after each addition. Add ground chicken, remove mixture from heat, and let cool slightly. Stiffly beat egg whites and fold into chicken mixture. Pour into soufflé dish and bake at 350 degrees for about 45 minutes until well puffed and browned. Garnish with crumbled bacon.

VARIATIONS

Curried Chicken Soufflé: Add 1½ teaspoons curry powder to basic recipe.

Chicken–Mushroom Soufflé: Add 3 ounce can mushroom stems and pieces, drained, when putting chicken through grinder.

Herb–Chicken Soufflé: Add 1 tablespoon fresh chopped herbs to basic recipe.

Chicken–Almond Soufflé: Add ¼ cup chopped toasted almonds to basic recipe.

COLD SALMON MOUSSE

Fresh salmon, although more expensive, is infinitely preferable to canned. Crabmeat, lobster, or shrimp can be substituted for salmon.

Type of dish: 1 quart mold, rinsed in cold water

Serves 4

2 cups fresh salmon, cooked (1 pound can, drained and boned)

1/4 tsp. cayenne pepper

1 tsp. seasoned salt

3 tbsp. lemon juice (preferably fresh)

1 envelope plain gelatin, softened in 1/2 cup cold water

3 tbsp. thick mayonnaise

1/4 cup heavy cream, stiffly whipped

2 tbsp. capers (optional)

thinly sliced unpeeled cucumber for garnish

Mash skinned, boned, cooked salmon with cayenne, seasoned salt, and lemon juice until mixture is smooth. Dissolve gelatin by setting dish of softened gelatin in a pan of hot water. Fold dissolved gelatin, mayonnaise, whipped cream, and capers into salmon mixture and blend well. Pour into mold and chill. Unmold just before serving and garnish with cucumber slices and mayonnaise.

KIPPERED HERRING SOUFFLÉ

Oven temperature: 350 degrees

Type of dish: 1½ quart soufflé dish, oiled

Serves 4–6

1 pair kippers, cooked and boned

4 ounce can stewed tomatoes (with onions and peppers), drained

1 clove garlic, mashed

2 tbsp. butter

¼ tsp. cayenne pepper

¾ cup milk

4 eggs, separated

1 egg white

½ tsp. dry mustard

1½ tbsp. grated Parmesan cheese

1 tbsp. chopped parsley

Combine kippers and stewed tomatoes and work into a rough puree. Gently brown garlic in butter and add cayenne, milk, egg yolks, dry mustard, and grated cheese. Heat thoroughly, stirring constantly. Fold in stiffly beaten egg whites, kipper/tomato mixture, and parsley, and pour into soufflé dish. Bake at 350 degrees until well puffed and browned, about 35 minutes.

MOUSSE DE MER

Type of dish: 2½–3 quart mold, oiled

Serves 8

2 envelopes plain gelatin
2 tbsp. cold water
¼ cup white wine
2 chicken stock cubes, dissolved in ¼ cup boiling water
1½ cups mixed seafood, cooked
6 ounce can sliced mushrooms, drained
½ cup canned pimento, chopped

3 tbsp. freeze-dried chives
1 tbsp. parsley, chopped
1 cup celery, chopped
1 tsp. seasoned salt
¼ tsp. white pepper
1 cup heavy mayonnaise
1 cup heavy cream, stiffly whipped
sliced cucumber, seeded black grapes, and watercress to garnish

Dissolve gelatin in cold water and wine. Pour in chicken stock cubes dissolved in boiling water and stir until gelatin is completely dissolved. Add all other ingredients (mayonnaise and cream last) and blend well. Pour into mold and chill. Unmold and garnish with cucumber slices, seeded black grapes, and watercress.

STEAMED FISH MOUSSE

This is a substantial hot fish mousse, best served with a creamed vegetable, such as creamed spinach or mushrooms, over it. It is steamed on top of the stove, rather than baked.

Type of dish: 1 quart greased mold, fitted onto a rack over hot water in a covered pan

Serves 6

1½ pounds of fresh fish, cod, perch, halibut, haddock (preferably a combination of fish), finely chopped
1 tsp. seasoned salt
dash of cayenne pepper

1 tbsp. freeze-dried chives
5 egg whites, stiffly beaten
1 cup heavy cream, stiffly whipped

Combine chopped fish, seasoned salt, cayenne, and chives. Fold in stiffly beaten egg whites and cream, and pour into greased mold. Place mold upon a rack in a covered pan and steam for about 30 minutes. Unmold and serve with a creamed vegetable and rice.

VEAL AND EGG MOUSSE

Type of dish: 1 quart mold, rinsed in cold water

Serves 6

2 envelopes plain gelatin
¼ cup dry sherry
1⅓ cups chicken con-
  sommé
2 eggs, separated
2 cups cooked veal,
  coarsely ground
2 hard-boiled eggs,
  chopped

1 tbsp. mild prepared
  mustard
1 tbsp. freeze-dried chives
6 black olives, chopped
½ tsp. seasoned pepper
1 cup heavy cream, stiffly
  whipped

Soften gelatin in sherry, add consommé, and heat over a low flame until gelatin is dissolved. Beat egg yolks and slowly add to gelatin mixture, continuously beating. Stiffly beat egg whites and fold with veal, hard-boiled eggs, mustard, chives, olives, seasoned pepper, and stiffly whipped cream. Pour into mold and chill. Unmold and garnish with a tomato salad.

HOT PÂTÉ MOUSSE

This is a very rich mousse, best served as an hors d'oeuvre.

Oven temperature: 350 degrees

Type of dish: 1 quart mold, oiled, set in pan of water

Serves 4–6

½ cup raw chicken, ground	½ tsp. seasoned salt
1 egg white, unbeaten	2 tsp. freeze-dried chives
4 ounce can pâté (with truffles, if possible)	¼ tsp. white pepper
2 mushrooms, coarsely chopped	½ cup heavy cream
	2 egg whites, stiffly beaten

Puree in blender or food mill chicken, egg white, and pâté. Fold in chopped mushrooms, seasonings, cream, and stiffly beaten egg whites and pour into oiled mold set in a pan of water. Bake at 350 degrees for about half an hour. Unmold and serve with a butter sauce flavored with sherry and sprinkle with chopped parsley.

HAM MOUSSE

The flavor of this mousse depends upon the quality of the ham used—leftover ham from a home-cooked ham is preferable to slices bought prepackaged.

Type of dish: 1 quart mold, rinsed in cold water

Serves 6

2 envelopes plain gelatin
¼ cup dry sherry
⅓ cup port
1 cup rich chicken consommé
2 large eggs, separated
3 cups cooked ham, roughly ground

2 tsp. Dijon or Bahamian mustard
¼ tsp. allspice
1 cup heavy cream, stiffly whipped
6–8 pickled mushrooms or artichoke hearts for garnish

In a saucepan, soften gelatin in sherry and port. Add consomme and heat until gelatin is dissolved. Remove from heat. Beat egg yolks and add to broth in a slow stream, beating as you add to avoid eggs becoming stringy. When blended, heat again over a low flame. Set aside when heated through. Stiffly beat egg whites and fold with ham, mustard, allspice, and stiffly whipped cream into broth mixture. Pour into mold and chill. Unmold and garnish with pickled mushrooms or artichokes.

VARIATIONS

Ham and Tomato Mousse: Add the meat of one large skinned tomato to the ham mixture before pouring into mold, and garnish mold with skinned tomato quarters.

Ham Mousse with Pineapple: Add three tablespoons of well-drained crushed pineapple to ham mixture before pouring into mold. Garnish mold with pineapple tidbits.

MOUSSE WITH CURED MEAT
(*Tongue, Corned Beef, Pastrami*)

Type of dish: 1 quart ring mold, oiled

Serves 4–6

1 envelope plain gelatin, softened in ¼ cup port
¾ cup consommé, heated
2½ cups well-chopped meat, as much fat as possible removed
¼ cup scallions, finely chopped
2 tbsp. green pepper, finely chopped
3 ounce can mushroom stems and pieces, drained
2 tbsp. fresh parsley, chopped
½ tsp. seasoned salt
½ tsp. lemon pepper
2 tsp. sharp prepared mustard
½ cup sour cream

Combine softened gelatin and heated consommé in a saucepan and heat over medium flame until gelatin has melted completely. Remove from flame. Combine all other ingredients up to sour cream in recipe listing and blend thoroughly. When gelatin is cooled and begins to jell, pour over meat mixture, coating all ingredients. Beat cream slightly and swirl through meat mixture, so you get a contrast of cream and meat. Do not mix thoroughly. Pour into mold and chill until completely set. Unmold and garnish lavishly.

SOUFFLÉ WITH CHIPPED BEEF

This soufflé is a variation on a Western omelette, with chipped beef and peppers making a casserole base, and a fluffy soufflé topping them.

Oven temperature: 375 degrees

Type of dish: 1½ quart soufflé dish, buttered

Serves 4

4 ounce package dried beef, rinsed twice in boiling water and drained
¼ cup butter
3 tbsp. flour
2 cups milk
¾ tsp. seasoned pepper
¼ tsp. dry mustard
2 tsp. Worcestershire sauce

½ green pepper, seeded and chopped fine
½ red pepper, seeded and chopped fine
3 ounce can chopped mushrooms, drained
¼ tsp. seasoned salt
3 eggs, separated
1 egg white

Combine dried beef and butter in a frying pan and frizzle beef until it begins to crisp. Add flour, milk, seasonings and cook over a medium heat, stirring constantly, until thick and smooth. Blend in peppers and mushrooms and pour mixture into buttered soufflé dish. Add seasoned salt to egg whites and beat until stiff. Beat egg yolks until lemon colored and fold into beaten egg whites. Pour mixture over chipped beef mixture and bake at 375 degrees for about 25 minutes until puffed and browned.

6

Cheese Soufflés

BASIC CHEESE SOUFFLÉ

Oven temperature: 375 degrees

Type of dish: 1½ quart soufflé dish, buttered

Serves 6

¼ cup butter	¾ cup grated Swiss cheese
¼ cup flour	¾ cup grated Parmesan cheese
2 cups milk	
½ tsp. salt	5 eggs, separated
¼ tsp. white pepper	1 egg white
pinch of nutmeg	

Whisk together butter and flour over medium heat until smooth and add milk, salt, pepper, and nutmeg. Continue whisking until thickened and smooth. Stir in cheeses and continue stirring until cheese is melted and the mixture is smooth. Remove from heat and whisk in egg yolks. Cool. Beat egg whites until stiff and fold quickly into cheese mixture. Pour into buttered soufflé dish and bake at 375 degrees for about 25 minutes, until well puffed and browned.

VARIATIONS

With Garlic Croutons: Sauté one clove of garlic in 2 tbsp. of olive oil. Add 2 slices of day-old bread, crusted and finely cubed, and sauté until browned. Drain and add to soufflé when folding in egg whites.

With Bacon: Fry two slices of bacon until crisp.

Drain well and crumble, adding to soufflé when folding in egg whites.

With Chives: Add 1 tbsp. freeze-dried or fresh chives when folding in egg whites.

CAMEMBERT OR BRIE SOUFFLÉ

The soft cheeses of France make marvelous soufflés, and enable you to utilize cheese that has not yet ripened sufficiently to be eaten on its own. Better still is the ripened cheese, if you can bear to give it up.

Oven temperature: 375 degrees

Type of dish: 1½ quart soufflé dish, buttered

Serves 4 generously

1 whole Camembert or Brie, about 6 inches in diameter
2 tbsp. butter
2 tbsp. flour
1 cup milk
1 tsp. freeze-dried shallot powder

½ tsp. salt
¼ tsp. white pepper
¼ tsp. paprika
5 eggs, separated
1 egg white

Peel Camembert or Brie carefully, taking off only as much of the outside crust as is dried and hardened. Finely dice remaining cheese. Whisk together butter and flour over medium heat until smooth and add milk, stirring until thickened. Remove from heat and stir in diced cheese, shallot powder, salt, pepper, and paprika. Keep stirring until cheese is melted—return to heat if necessary briefly. Drop in egg yolks one by one, stirring after each addition. Stiffly beat egg whites and fold into cheese mixture. Pour into greased soufflé dish and bake at 375 degrees for about 45 minutes until puffed and well browned.

CHEDDAR CHEESE SOUFFLÉ

Cheddar cheese soufflé has the most pronounced flavor of all the cheese soufflés, and lends itself best to the addition of bacon or ham.

Oven temperature: 325 degrees

Type of dish: 1½ quart soufflé dish, buttered

Serves 4

3 tbsp. butter
¼ cup flour
1 cup milk
½ tsp. seasoned salt
¼ tsp. dry mustard
dash of cayenne pepper

1 cup sharp cheddar cheese, grated (about 4 ounces)
4 eggs, separated
1 egg white

Blend together butter and flour in a saucepan over medium heat, then add milk, salt, mustard, and cayenne. Continue stirring until sauce is thickened and smooth. Lower heat and add grated cheddar cheese and continue stirring until cheese is completely melted. Remove from heat and whisk in egg yolks, one at a time. Stiffly beat egg whites and fold cheese mixture into egg whites. Pour into buttered soufflé dish and bake at 325 degrees for about 1 hour until puffed and well browned.

SWISS CHEESE SOUFFLÉ

This soufflé has a nutty flavor and is a delicious change from the basic cheese soufflé.

Oven temperature: 325 degrees

Type of dish: 2 quart soufflé dish, buttered

Serves 6

¼ cup butter
¼ cup flour
1½ cups milk
1 tsp. salt
¼ tsp. nutmeg
dash of cayenne pepper

2 cups natural Swiss cheese, grated (about 8 ounces)
5 eggs, separated
1 egg white

Blend together butter and flour in a saucepan over medium heat, then add milk, salt, nutmeg, and cayenne. Continue stirring until sauce is thickened and smooth. Lower heat and add grated Swiss cheese and continue stirring until cheese has completely melted. Remove from heat and whisk in egg yolks, one at a time. Stiffly beat egg whites and fold cheese mixture into egg whites. Pour into greased soufflé dish and bake at 325 degrees for about 1¼ hours or until puffed and well browned.

CORN AND CHEESE SOUFFLÉ

This is a fine choice for luncheon menus. If you can find white corn, either frozen or canned, try it rather than yellow corn.

Oven temperature: 350 degrees

Type of dish: 1½ quart soufflé dish, greased, set in pan of hot water

Serves 6

¼ cup butter
¼ cup flour
2 cups milk, at room temperature
½ tsp. seasoned salt
¼ tsp white pepper
1 tsp. freeze-dried chives

1 cup cheddar cheese, grated
4 large eggs, separated
1 egg white
2 boxes frozen corn (or 1½ cups canned whole corn, drained)

In a saucepan, melt butter over low heat and whisk in flour to make a smooth roux. Slowly pour in milk and continue whisking until you have a smooth sauce. Add salt, pepper, and chives, then cheese. Continue blending until cheese has melted. Remove from heat. Beat egg yolks and add to cheese mixture with corn. Stiffly beat egg whites and quickly fold into cheese mixture. Pour into soufflé dish, and set dish into a pan of hot water. Bake at 350 degrees for about 1 hour. Serve immediately.

7

Vegetable Mousses & Soufflés

TOMATO MOUSSE

This mousse makes a splendid ring, to be filled with chicken or tuna salad, or a mold to which you add bits of chopped raw vegetable.

Type of dish: 1 quart mold

Serves 4–6

10 medium tomatoes, halved, peeled, seeded, juice reserved	¼ cup white wine
	1 tbsp. tomato catsup
½ tsp. seasoned salt	¾ cup heavy cream, whipped
¼ tsp. white pepper	½ cup mayonnaise
2 tbsp. plain gelatin	

Puree tomato pulp in food mill or blender. Add enough of reserved juice to it to make two cups and season with salt and pepper. Soften gelatin in wine, then set bowl in a pan of hot water to dissolve the gelatin. Combine tomato, gelatin, and catsup and work through a sieve to remove any big pieces. Fold in whipped cream and mayonnaise and pour into mold. Chill until firmly set. Unmold and fill as desired.

AVOCADO MOUSSE

This pale green mousse is marvelous made in a ring and filled with baby shrimp in a mustard mayonnaise.

Type of dish: 1 quart ring mold, rinsed in cold water

Serves 4

1 tbsp. plain gelatin	2 avocado pears
¼ cup cold water	1 tbsp. lemon juice
1 chicken stock cube, dissolved in 1 cup hot water	½ cup thick mayonnaise
	½ cup sour cream
	½ tsp. seasoned salt
1 tsp. sugar	dash of Tabasco

Soften gelatin in cold water, add hot chicken stock and sugar. Stir and allow to cool. Mash avocado pears with lemon juice, mayonnaise, sour cream, seasoned salt, and Tabasco. When well blended, stir in setting gelatin and blend again well. Pour into ring mold and chill thoroughly until set. Unmold and fill as desired.

HOT VEGETABLE SOUFFLÉS

(Celery, Carrot, Broccoli, Asparagus, Spinach, Cauliflower, Pea, Corn, Mushroom)

These soufflés are best made in a ring mold, to be filled with another vegetable, usually buttered or creamed for contrast. While I think vegetable soufflés are nicest using freshly cooked vegetables, leftover vegetables will certainly suffice.

Oven temperature: 350 degrees

Type of dish: Buttered ring mold, or 1 quart soufflé dish, set in a pan of hot water

Serves 4–6

3 tbsp. butter	1/2 tsp. nutmeg
3 tbsp. flour	3 eggs, separated
1/2 tsp. seasoned salt	1 cup cooked vegetable,
1/4 tsp. white pepper	mashed
1 cup hot half-and-half	1 tbsp. freeze-dried chives

In a saucepan, melt butter and stir in flour, pepper, and salt. When whisked smooth, add hot half-and-half and nutmeg and continue stirring until a thick smooth sauce is obtained. Remove from heat and drop egg yolks into sauce, whisking after each addition. Add the mashed vegetable and chives, then fold in stiffly beaten egg whites. Pour into buttered ring mold set in a pan of hot water. Bake at 350 degrees until well puffed and browned. Let sit for 5 minutes before running knife around the edges to unmold onto a hot platter. Fill as desired.

POTATO SOUFFLÉ

Oven temperature: 375 degrees

Type of dish: 1½ quart soufflé dish, buttered

Serves 4–6

2 eggs, separated
2 cups mashed potatoes
½ cup cheddar cheese, grated
¼ cup milk
2 tbsp. freeze-dried chives
2 tbsp. melted butter
dash of Worcestershire sauce
1 tsp. seasoned salt
¼ tsp. seasoned pepper
almond slivers or sliced almonds for garnish

Mix together all ingredients except egg whites and almonds. Stiffly beat egg whites and fold into potato mixture. Pour into buttered soufflé dish, top with almonds, and bake at 375 degrees for about 30 minutes, or until soufflé is puffed and well browned.

SWEET POTATO SOUFFLÉ

This is a superb soufflé to accompany ham or tongue.

Oven temperature: 400 degrees

Type of dish: 1½ quart soufflé dish, greased

Serves 4–6

2 cups cooked sweet potatoes, mashed
1 cup sour cream
¼ cup softened butter
1 tsp. ground cinnamon
½ tsp. ground allspice
½ tsp. ground nutmeg
½ tsp. seasoned salt
dash cayenne pepper
¼ cup brandy
grated rind of 1 orange
5 eggs, separated
1 egg white

Cream together sweet potatoes, sour cream, and butter until smooth. Add seasonings, brandy, and orange rind, then egg yolks. Blend thoroughly. Beat egg whites until stiff and fold into potato mixture. Pour into greased soufflé dish and bake at 400 degrees for about 30 minutes until well puffed and browned.

ONION SOUFFLÉ

Oven temperature: 350 degrees

Type of dish: 1½ quart soufflé dish, buttered

Serves 4–6

3 tbsp. butter
3 tbsp. flour
¼ tsp. nutmeg
½ tsp. seasoned salt
¼ tsp. white pepper
¾ cup milk
5 eggs, separated
1 egg white

3 white onions, thinly sliced and browned in butter
2 tbsp. sweet vermouth
crumbled bacon and chopped parsley for garnish (optional)

Combine butter, flour, and seasonings and whisk over hot water until smooth. Add milk and stir over medium heat until a thick sauce is obtained. Add egg yolks, browned onions, and vermouth. Remove from heat and add stiffly beaten egg whites. Pour into greased soufflé dish and bake at 350 degrees for about 35 minutes until well puffed and browned. Sprinkle with crumbled bacon and chopped parsley.

TOMATO SOUFFLÉ

Oven temperature: 350 degrees

Type of dish: 1 quart soufflé dish, greased

Serves 4

1 cup stewed tomatoes (8 ounce can), with onions and peppers	¼ tsp. seasoned pepper
	3 tbsp. flour
	3 eggs, separated
3 tbsp. butter	¼ cup Parmesan cheese
1 tsp. seasoned salt	1 tsp. dried parsley

Sieve tomatoes in food mill or blender. Melt butter in a saucepan, add salt, pepper, and flour and blend. Add tomatoes and cook over medium heat until thickened. Be sure to stir constantly or the mixture will burn. Remove from heat. Beat egg yolks thoroughly and add to tomatoes. Beat egg whites until stiff and fold into tomato mixture. Sprinkle with grated cheese and parsley. Pour into greased soufflé dish and bake at 350 degrees about 25 minutes until well puffed and browned.

8

Sweet Mousses & Soufflés

HOT PRUNE WHIP MOUSSE

This recipe is also delicious when made with a combination of dry fruits—apricots, prunes, currants.

Oven temperature: 300 degrees

Type of dish: 2 quart soufflé dish, greased, set in pan of hot water

Serves 4

1 cup stewed fruit, pitted
   and drained
½ cup brown sugar
1 tbsp. flour
1 tbsp. lemon juice
rind of one lemon, finely
   grated

½ tsp. allspice
4 egg whites
½ tsp. cream of tartar
¼ cup white sugar

Sieve fruit (using some of its juice if necessary) in a food mill or blender, add brown sugar, and cook over low heat until the consistency of thick jam. Add flour, lemon juice, rind, and allspice and blend well. Set aside. Beat egg whites with cream of tartar until stiff and dust in white sugar when soft peaks form. Fold prune mixtures into egg mixture and pour into greased soufflé dish. Bake at 300 degrees in pan of hot water for about 1½ hours. Serve hot with cold heavy cream, or cold with custard sauce.

COFFEE MOUSSE

This is a very rich and, when decorated, extremely impressive dessert.

Type of dish: 2 quart mold, rinsed in cold water.

Serves 8

2 tbsp. plain gelatin	¼ cup brandy
2 cups cold coffee	1 tsp. vanilla
2 tbsp. instant espresso coffee powder	1 cup heavy cream, whipped
3 eggs, separated	shaved chocolate, toasted almonds, whipped cream for garnish
½ to ¾ cups sugar (adjust to taste)	

Soften gelatin in cold coffee, then combine in the top of a double boiler with instant coffee powder, egg yolks, and sugar. Cook, stirring constantly, until gelatin is completely dissolved and mixture is thickening. Remove from heat, and allow to cool. When coffee is cooled and thickened, add brandy and vanilla. Beat egg whites until stiff. Combine coffee mixture, beaten egg whites, and stiffly whipped cream and pour into mold, chilling until set. Unmold, and decorate lavishly with shaved chocolate, almonds, and whipped cream.

FRESH ORANGE MOUSSE

Type of dish: Glass serving dish
Serves 6

1 tbsp. plain gelatin	1 tbsp. lemon juice
¼ cup cold water	Peel of one orange, finely
3 eggs, separated	grated
⅓ cup sugar	1 can mandarin oranges,
juice from 3 medium	drained, for decoration
oranges	

Soften gelatin in cold water, then set dish in pan of
hot water to dissolve, stirring frequently. Combine
egg yolks, sugar, juices, and peel, blending well.
Whisk in melted gelatin and continue whisking until
mixture begins to thicken. Stiffly beat egg whites and
fold orange mixture into them. Pour into serving
dish and chill. Garnish with mandarin orange slices
before serving.

CHOCOLATE MOUSSE

Type of dish: 1½ quart serving dish

Serves 6

8 ounces semi-sweet chocolate, melted
¼ cup brandy
1½ tsp. vanilla extract
8 egg whites
dash of salt

½ cup sugar, Verifine preferred
whipped cream, shaved bitter chocolate, and sliced almonds for garnish

Combine cooled melted chocolate, brandy, and vanilla extract, and mix thoroughly. Beat egg whites with salt until stiff and slowly add sugar, continuing beating until very stiff and glossy. Fold chocolate mixture into egg whites and pour into serving dish. Chill until serving time. Garnish with whipped cream, shaved bitter chocolate, and sliced almond.

VARIATIONS

Chocolate Chip Chocolate Mousse: Dice half a package of chocolate chips into fine bits and add when adding egg whites.

Orange Chocolate Mousse: Substitute Grand Marnier for brandy and add 1 tbsp. finely grated orange rind when adding egg whites.

Mocha Mousse: Substitute coffee liqueur for brandy.

Chocolate Mint Mousse: Substitute creme de menthe for brandy.

CARAMEL MOUSSE

This is a rich, smooth, and delicate mousse, wonderful when made in a ring and filled with marrons.

Type of dish: 1 quart mold, oiled

Serves 4

1 cup sugar
¼ cup water
3 eggs
2 egg yolks
½ cup heavy cream, lightly whipped

1 tbsp. plain gelatin
juice of 1 lemon increased to ¼ cup with water
marrons and whipped cream for garnish

In a heavy pan—cast iron is best—heat ¾ cup sugar with very little water until sugar has melted and cooks to a golden caramel. Carefully add ¼ cup water and stir well. Remove from heat and pour into a bowl to cool. Whisk together eggs, egg yolks, and remaining sugar. Set bowl with caramel in a pan of ice and add lightly whipped cream, blending them well. Dissolve gelatin in lemon juice and water in a pan of hot water until completely melted. Stir together eggs, caramel, and gelatin, and whisk until the mixture begins to thicken. Pour into oiled mold and chill until firm. Fill or garnish with marrons and whipped cream.

APPLE AND WALNUT MOUSSE

Type of dish: 1½ quart pretty serving dish, preferably glass

Serves 6

2 pounds tart cooking apples, peeled and cored
rind and juice of 1 large lemon
3 tbsp. cider
⅔ cup sugar
1 or 2 drops green food coloring

1 tbsp. plain gelatin
2 eggs, separated
1 tbsp. cornstarch
1 cup milk
1 tsp. vanilla extract
1 cup heavy cream
1 package walnuts, finely chopped

Combine apples, rind of half lemon, cut in strips, and cider in a saucepan. Cover and cook over low heat until apples are soft. Stir often to keep from burning. Remove from heat, extract lemon rind and discard. When cooled, puree with ½ cup sugar and add food coloring. Add gelatin to lemon juice and leave to soften. Combine rest of sugar, egg yolks, cornstarch, and milk in a saucepan over low heat until thickened. Remove from heat and add softened gelatin, apple puree, and vanilla. Lightly whip the heavy cream and stiffly beat egg whites. Combine, and then fold apple mixture into them. Pour into serving dish and chill until set. Sprinkle with chopped walnuts. For best flavor, this mousse should be removed from the refrigerator at least an hour before serving.

BANANA MOUSSE

The delicate smoothness of this mousse makes a perfect combination with berries or fruit salad to which a fruit-based liqueur has been added.

Type of dish: 1 quart mold; if filling with fruit salad, ring mold, rinsed in cold water

Serves 6

1 cup light cream	1½ cups heavy cream
2 tbsp. sugar	½ tsp. vanilla extract
1 envelope plain gelatin	½ tsp. brandy extract
¼ cup milk	2 large ripe bananas,
2 egg yolks, beaten	mashed

Combine light cream and sugar in the top of a double boiler and scald. Add gelatin to milk to soften. Add egg yolks and heavy cream to scalded light cream, stirring constantly until thickened. Remove from heat and add softened gelatin, stirring until dissolved. Add extracts and mashed bananas, blend thoroughly, and turn into mold. Chill until firm, preferably overnight. Unmold before serving and garnish with fruit.

FROZEN MAPLE MOUSSE

Type of dish: 6 cup mold, suitable for freezer

Serves 6

 1 cup pure maple syrup
 4 eggs, separated
 2 cups heavy cream, stiffly whipped
 chopped unsalted nuts for garnish

Combine syrup and egg yolks in top of a double boiler and cook until smooth and thickened. Set aside. Stiffly beat egg whites and fold in whipped cream. Beat egg/syrup mixture until fluffy and fold in whipped cream and egg whites. Pour into mold, dust with chopped nuts, and freeze until serving time.

RASPBERRY OR BLACKBERRY MOUSSE

A combination of berries gives this mousse an unusual flavor.

Type of dish: Deep glass serving dish

Serves 6

1 pound fresh berries (or
  2 15-ounce cans,
  drained)
½ cup heavy cream,
  stiffly beaten
½ cup sugar (adjust ac-
  cording to sweetness of
  fruit)

1 tbsp. plain gelatin
3 tbsp. orange juice
  (preferably fresh)
2 egg whites, stiffly beaten
whipped cream and con-
  fectioners' sugar for
  garnish

Reserve several perfect berries to garnish the top of the mousse. Sieve the rest of the berries to make about 1 cup of puree, and mix with heavy cream and sugar. Dissolve gelatin in orange juice by setting bowl in a large bowl of hot water, stirring constantly. When dissolved, add gelatin to berry puree and stir well. Fold in stiffly beaten egg whites. Pour into deep glass serving dish and chill until set. When set, decorate with whole berries, whipped cream, and a sprinkling of confectioners' sugar.

FROZEN CITRUS MOUSSE
  (Orange, Lemon or Lime)

Because this mousse uses quite a lot of grated rind, be sure to pick fruit with smooth, highly colored rind.

Type of dish: 1½ quart mold, rinsed in cold water

Serves 6

> 3 limes or lemons, or 2 medium oranges and juice of 1 lemon
> 1½ cups sugar
> 2 cups milk
> 2 cups heavy cream, stiffly beaten

Grate the rind of the fruit, reserving about 1½ tbsp. (keep in foil or plastic wrap, tightly sealed, in the refrigerator). Squeeze juice and add to rind, add sugar, and slowly add milk. Fold this into the stiffly beaten cream and pour quickly into mold. Freeze. About an hour after putting in freezer, remove and blend thoroughly so as to combine iced parts with unfrozen center. Return to refrigerator to freeze again. Just before serving, unmold and sprinkle with reserved rind.

FROZEN STRAWBERRY OR RASPBERRY MOUSSE

Type of dish: 1½ quart mold, rinsed in cold water
Serves 6

3 packages frozen berries, defrosted and drained
3 tbsp. sugar
2 tbsp. kirsch
2 tbsp. cointreau

2 egg whites
pinch of salt
2 cups heavy cream, stiffly whipped

Pick out three whole strawberries or six raspberries and reserve as garnish. Puree the remainder of the berries in a blender or food mill. Strain to remove seeds. Combine the seedless puree with 1 tablespoon sugar and liqueurs and set aside. Beat egg whites with salt until peaks form and then slowly add 2 tbsp. sugar, continuing beating until stiff. Fold in puree and stiffly whipped cream. Pour into decorative mold, cover with foil or plastic wrap, and freeze until solid. Remove shortly before serving, unmold, and decorate with reserved berries.

BASIC SWEET SOUFFLÉ

This is the basic recipe for a sweet soufflé, to be varied by either lining the soufflé dish with fruit or liqueur-soaked sponge, or by the addition of flavoring to the recipe itself.

Oven temperature: 400 degrees

Type of dish: 1½ quart soufflé dish, buttered

Serves 6

3 tbsp. butter	¼ cup sugar
3 tbsp. flour	1 tbsp. vanilla extract
¾ cup hot milk	pinch of salt
4 eggs, separated	1 tbsp. sugar
1 egg white	confectioners' sugar

Combine butter and flour in a saucepan and whisk until blended. Pour in hot milk and whisk over medium heat until thickened. Remove from heat and drop in egg yolks one at a time, and continue whisking until custard is thick. Add ¼ cup sugar and extract. Beat egg whites with a pinch of salt until they hold their shape. Sprinkle with 1 tbsp. sugar and continue beating until stiff. Fold meringue into cooled custard and pour into buttered soufflé dish. Reduce oven temperature to 375 degrees and bake for about 40 minutes until well puffed and browned. Sprinkle lavishly with confectioners' sugar.

Almond Soufflé: Use 1 tsp. vanilla and 1 tsp. almond extract in basic recipe. Fold in 1/3 cup ground almonds with egg whites.

Apricot Soufflé: Add 1 cup apricot puree to basic recipe and substitute 1 tsp. almond extract for vanilla extract in basic recipe.

Coffee Soufflé: Add 2 tsp. instant coffee powder to hot milk before making custard and substitute 1 tsp. brandy extract for vanilla.

Fruit Soufflé: Line soufflé dish with 2 cups of sliced fruit, sweetened and marinated overnight in kirsch, cointreau, maraschino, or Grand Marnier. Drain before using, reserving liqueur to make a sauce to serve with soufflé.

Or Add 1 cup pureed fruit, flavored with liqueur, to the egg yolks when making custard.

Liqueur-Bottomed Soufflé: Line soufflé dish with sponge, ladyfingers, macaroons, or angel food cake that has been soaked in rum or liqueur. The cake should not be drowned but thoroughly moistened.

Spice Soufflé: Add 1/2 tsp. each ground cinnamon, nutmeg, and allspice to the basic recipe.

CITRUS SOUFFLÉS
(Orange, Lemon, Lime, or Tangerine)

This is a light and refreshing soufflé. Use limes and tangerines only at the height of their availability for the best yield in juice and flavor.

Oven temperature: 325 degrees

Type of dish: 1½ quart soufflé dish, buttered, set in a pan of hot water

Serves 6

> 6 large eggs, separated
> 1 egg white
> 1 cup sugar
> juice and rind of 1 large lemon; or rind of 1 orange, ⅓ cup fresh orange juice, plus 1 tbsp. lemon juice; or rind and juice of 2 limes; or rind of two tangerines (if small, otherwise 1 large), ⅓ cup tangerine juice, plus 1 tbsp. lemon juice
> confectioners' sugar

Combine egg yolks and sugar and beat foamy and lemon colored. Add juice and rind, then stiffly beaten egg whites. Pour into greased soufflé dish, set in pan of hot water, and bake at 325 degrees for about 1 hour, until well puffed and browned. Dust with confectioners' sugar.

NUT SOUFFLÉ

A combination of nuts makes the most interesting flavor for this delicately flavored soufflé. This is a soufflé made most delicious by the addition of a sauce, such as brandy, rum, or mocha sauce.

Oven temperature: 325 degrees

Type of dish: 1½ quart soufflé dish, buttered, set in a pan of hot water

Serves 4

3 eggs, separated	1 cup milk
1 egg white	¾ cup mixed unsalted nuts, finely ground (pecans, almonds, hazelnuts)
3 tbsp. flour	
4 tbsp. sugar	
1 tsp. nutmeg	
¼ tsp. salt	3 tbsp. melted butter

Beat egg yolks and combine with flour and sugar, nutmeg and salt in the top of a double boiler. When blended, pour in milk and stir over medium heat until thick. Add ground nuts and butter, and remove from heat. Fold in stiffly beaten egg whites and pour mixture into buttered soufflé dish set in a pan of hot water. Bake at 325 degrees for about 1 hour, until well puffed and browned.

CHOCOLATE SOUFFLÉ

Oven temperature: 325 degrees

Type of dish: 1½ quart soufflé dish, greased, set in a pan of hot water

Serves 6

2 tbsp. butter
4 tbsp. flour
1 cup milk
¼ cup water
⅓ cup sugar

2 squares Baker's un-
    sweetened chocolate
4 eggs, separated
1 egg white

In a saucepan melt butter and whisk in flour. Slowly pour in milk and whisk together over medium heat until thick and smooth. Remove from heat. Combine water, sugar, and chocolate in a saucepan and stir over medium heat until chocolate is melted. Cool. Combine cream sauce, chocolate sauce, and egg yolks. Beat until smooth. Fold in stiffly beaten egg whites and pour into greased soufflé dish set in pan of hot water. Bake at 325 degrees for about 45 minutes, until soufflé is well puffed and browned.

VARIATIONS

Chocolate Rum Soufflé: Add 1 tsp. rum extract to the basic recipe.

Chocolate Orange Soufflé: Add finely grated rind of an orange to basic recipe.

ORANGE MARMALADE SOUFFLÉ

This soufflé is steamed in the top of a double boiler, rather than baked in the oven, and served with its own sauce.

Type of dish: Large double boiler, top part well greased

Serves 6

4 eggs, separated
¼ cup sugar
¼ tsp. salt
¼ cup marmalade (fine-cut imported marmalade preferred)
½ cup sugar
1 tbsp. cornstarch
¾ cup milk

2 tbsp. kirsch or Grand Marnier
2 tbsp. brandy
1 cup orange juice (fresh, if possible)
2 tbsp. freshly grated orange rind
1 can mandarin oranges, drained

Beat egg whites well, adding ¼ cup of sugar and salt when foamy, and continue beating until stiff. Fold in marmalade. Pour into top of double boiler. Cover and steam over bottom part of double boiler for about 45 to 50 minutes.

In the top of another double boiler, blend together ½ cup sugar, cornstarch, milk, liqueurs, brandy, orange juice and rind. Cook until thick and smooth. Remove from heat and add mandarin orange slices. When soufflé is cooked, unmold, pour sauce around it, and serve immediately.

LIQUEUR SOUFFLÉS

(Grand Marnier, Tia Maria, Cointreau, Kirsch, Benedictine)

Delicately flavored liqueur soufflés are a really festive ending to a meal. They may be served plain, sprinkled with confectioners' sugar, or with a warm, light, fruity sauce (see page 18).

Oven temperature: 350 degrees

Type of dish: 1 quart soufflé dish, buttered

Serves 6

⅓ cup flour
½ cup sugar
½ cup milk
1 tbsp. butter (unsalted preferable)

¼ cup liqueur
3 egg yolks, beaten
6 egg whites, stiffly beaten

Combine flour and sugar in a saucepan and over low heat pour in milk, whisking as you pour. Cook, stirring constantly, until smooth and thick. Set aside and whisk in butter and liqueur. Fold stiffly beaten egg whites into egg yolk mixture and pour into buttered soufflé dish. Bake at 350 degrees for 20 minutes, then increase oven to 400 degrees for another 15 minutes, until soufflé is puffed and well browned.

ICED STRAWBERRY SOUFFLÉ

This is a sumptuous dessert, at its best served at the height of the strawberry season, when the fruit is at its peak, in both color and flavor. For optimum results, do not use frozen berries.

Type of dish: 1½ quart soufflé dish, with at least a 2 inch collar

Serves 6

2 pounds strawberries, hulled and washed	1 cup Verifine sugar
2 rounded tbsp. plain gelatin	juice from two lemons, well strained
¼ cup cold water	3 egg whites
	1 cup heavy cream

Pick over strawberries and reserve several perfect berries. Put the rest in an electric blender or food mill and puree—there should be about 3 cups of puree. Soak gelatin in cold water to soften. In a saucepan combine half the puree with ½ cup sugar, gelatin, and lemon juice. Over a low heat, never allowing to boil, heat mixture until the gelatin is completely dissolved. Stir continuously. Remove from heat and add remaining puree. Beat egg whites until stiff, adding sugar until stiff peaks form. Beat heavy cream until peaks begin to hold shape, and fold, with egg whites, into puree. Pour into collared soufflé dish and chill until set. Gently remove collar (see p. 14) and decorate top and sides of soufflé with sliced berries. Dust top with confectioners' sugar just before serving.

Index

Almond-Chicken Soufflé, 30
Almond Soufflé, 70
Apple and Walnut Mousse,
    63
Apricot Soufflé, 70
Avocado Mousse, 51

bacon, cheese soufflé with, 42–
    43
Banana Mousse, 64
beef, chipped, soufflé with, 40
Blackberry Mousse, 66
Brie Soufflé, 44

Camembert Soufflé, 44
Caramel Mousse, 62
Cheddar Cheese Soufflé, 45
Cheese Soufflé
    with bacon, 42–43
    basic, 42
    camembert or brie, 44
    cheddar, 45
    with chives, 43
    corn and, 47
    with garlic croutons, 42

Swiss, 46
Chicken-Almond Soufflé, 30
Chicken Curry Mousse, cold,
    28
Chicken-Herb Soufflé, 30
Chicken-Mushroom Soufflé, 30
Chicken Soufflé, 29
chilling mousses and soufflés,
    11
chipped beef, soufflé with, 40
chives, cheese soufflé with, 43
Chocolate Chip Chocolate
    Mousse, 61
Chocolate Mint Mousse, 61
Chocolate Mousse, 61
Chocolate Orange Soufflé, 73
Chocolate Rum Soufflé, 73
Chocolate Soufflé, 73
Citrus Mousse, frozen, 67
Citrus Soufflés, 71
Coffee Mousse, 59
Coffee Soufflé, 70
Cold Chicken Curry Mousse,
    28
Cold Duck and Orange
    Mousse, 26
Cold Poultry Mousse, 27

Cold Salmon Mousse, 31
collars, making soufflés and, 6
Corn and Cheese Soufflé, 47
cured meat, mousse with, 39
Curried Chicken Soufflé, 29

decorating mousses and soufflés, 14–15, 18–19
dishes
  for mousses, 9
  for soufflés, 5–6
Duck and Orange Mousse, cold, 26

Egg and Veal Mousse, 35
eggs, 8–9
equipment, soufflé-making, 7–9

Fish Mousse, steamed, 34
Fresh Orange Mousse, 60
Frozen Citrus Mousse, 67
Frozen Maple Mousse, 65
Frozen Raspberry Mousse, 68
Frozen Strawberry Mousse, 68
fruit-jam sauce, 18
Fruit Soufflé, 70

garlic croutons, cheese soufflé with, 42
gelatin, mousse-making and, 10–11

Ham Mousse, 37
Ham Mousse with Pineapple, 38
Ham and Tomato Mousse, 37–38
Herb-Chicken Soufflé, 30
Hot Pâté Mousse, 36
Hot Prune Whip Mousse, 58
Hot Vegetable Soufflés, 52

Iced Strawberry Soufflé, 76

jam-fruit sauce, 18

keeping mousses and soufflés, 22
Kippered Herring Soufflé, 32

lemon. See Citrus Mousse and Citrus Soufflés
lime. See Citrus Mousse and Citrus Soufflés
Liqueur-Bottomed Soufflé, 70
Liqueur Soufflés, 75

Maple Mousse, frozen, 65
meat, cured, mousse with, 39
Mocha Mousse, 61
molds, mousse, 9
mousse, savory
  avocado, 51

mousse, savory (*continued*)
chicken curry, cold, 28
with cured meat, 39
duck and orange, cold, 26
fish, steamed, 34
ham, 37
pâté, hot, 36
poultry, cold, 27
salmon, cold, 31
seafood, 33
tomato, 50
veal and egg, 35
mousse, sweet
apple and walnut, 63
banana, 64
blackberry, 66
caramel, 62
chocolate, 61
chocolate chip chocolate, 61
chocolate mint, 61
citrus, frozen, 67
coffee, 59
maple, frozen, 65
mocha, 61
orange, fresh, 60
orange chocolate, 61
prune whip, hot, 58
raspberry, 66
raspberry, frozen, 68
strawberry, frozen, 68
Mousse with Cured Meat, 39
Mousse de Mer, 33
mousses
chilling, 11
decorating, 14–15
gelatin in, 10–11
keeping, 22
making, basic rules for, 9–11
molds for, 9
sauces for, 18–19
serving, 14–15, 18–19
soufflés vs., 5
unmolding, 10
Mushroom-Chicken Soufflé, 30

Nut Soufflé, 72

Onion Soufflé, 55
Orange Chocolate Mousse, 61
Orange Marmalade Soufflé, 74
Orange Mousse, fresh, 60
Orange Soufflé, Chocolate, 73
ovens, 5, 9

Pâté Mousse, hot, 36
pineapple, ham mousse with, 38
pineapple, mousse-making and, 10
Potato Soufflé, 53
Poultry Mousse, cold, 27
Prune Whip Mousse, hot, 58

Raspberry Mousse, 66
frozen, 68
refrigeration, 22

reheating, 22
rum sauce, 18
Rum Soufflé, Chocolate, 73

Salmon Mousse, cold, 31
sauces, 18–19
  fruit-jam, 18
  rum, 18
  zabaglione, 18
seafood (Mousse de Mer), 33
serving mousses and soufflés, 14–15
soufflé, savory
  camembert or brie, 44
  cheddar cheese, 45
  cheese, basic, 42
  chicken, 29
  with chipped beef, 40
  corn and cheese, 47
  kippered herring, 32
  onion, 55
  potato, 53
  sweet potato, 54
  Swiss cheese, 46
  tomato, 56
  vegetable, 52
soufflé, sweet
  almond, 70
  apricot, 70
  basic, 69
  chocolate, 73
  chocolate orange, 73
  chocolate rum, 73
  citrus, 71

coffee, 70
fruit, 70
liqueur, 75
liqueur-bottomed, 70
nut, 72
orange marmalade, 74
spice, 70
strawberry, iced, 76
Soufflé with Chipped Beef, 40
soufflés
  collars and, 6
  decorating, 14–15
  dishes for, 5–6
  equipment for making, 7–9
  keeping, 22
  making, basic rules for, 5–9
  mousses vs., 5
  sauces for, 18–19
  savory, 4
  serving, 14–15, 18–19
  sweet, 4–5
Spice Soufflé, 70
Steamed Fish Mousse, 34
Strawberry Mousse, 68
Strawberry Soufflé, iced, 76
Sweet Potato Soufflé, 54
Swiss Cheese Soufflé, 46

tangerine. See Citrus Mousse and Citrus Soufflés
Tomato and Ham Mousse, 37

Tomato Mousse, 50

Tomato Soufflé, 56

unmolding, mousse-making and, 10

utensils, soufflé-making, 7–9

Veal and Egg Mousse, 35

Vegetable Soufflés, hot, 52

zabaglione sauce, 18

About the Author

Patricia Holden White is the author of two earlier cookbooks: *Cookies* (1968) and *Pie!* (1969). A former editor at a New York publishing house, she is now a literary agent in London.